6 STEPS GOALS TO ACTION

Your Strategy Manual

MAARTEN J.L. VAN HASSELT

Third Edition

Figures: Most pictures from MvH, Pexels, iStock, or Shutterstock
Paid as part of trial subscription ten free pictures

Cover and Interior Design by Chris Berge (bergedesign.com)

ISBN: 9789083404004 (Paperback)
ISBN: 9789083404011 (Ebook)

www.sixsteps-goals-action.com

This manual stands on its own. With complex projects, you may need more tools. Therefore, you will find references to examples, books and articles in "Tools and Techniques" ("T and T") at *https://sixteps-goals-action.com*.

THE SIX STEPS ARE FOR YOU.

The Six Steps are based on real-life, practical experience and will provide you with tools and techniques that have been proven to work in many strategic projects in a variety of roles and situations:

✓ ***Leading a business unit after a promotion.***
When taking over in any leadership role, you want to review existing plans and probably make your own strategic plan.

✓ ***A student analyzing a business case to present in class.***
When working on a case study and presenting a plan of action.

✓ ***An intern starting an assignment.***
The Six Steps will give structure to your project and help plan for your own development. As an intern, you will provide a fresh pair of eyes.

✓ ***A GP taking over from a retiring medical practice owner.***
Even though your predecessor ran a good practice, when you take over, you will have ideas about how to do things differently. The Six Steps will help you to structure this new approach.

✓ ***A politician seeing that vision and mission don't get results.***
You hear that your voters want action. Design the steps to achieve goals and maintain support.

✓ ***An entrepreneur convincing an investor to finance your start-up.***
An investor wants to see a strategy and how you will make money. The Six Steps makes sure you don't forget areas, and you will be more convincing.

✓ ***A professional planning the first thirty, sixty, and ninety days of a new job.***
A new job is your most important project. Working backward from your goals, you will be able to make an action plan to cross barriers and to create value for yourself and your employers.

✓ ***An adviser or consultant contracted by a client.***
A client brings you in from outside because a plan to create value is missing or the existing strategy didn't give the required results. A robust process keeps you and the organization's resources on track.

✓ ***A parent organizing a dinner party.***
Many things need to happen in the right sequence, from inviting people and buying ingredients all the way to making sure everyone gets home safely. Make a plan: the dinner strategy!

✓ ***A student thinking about career planning.***

You have a goal; you need a plan to cross the barriers.What is the goal? What is the end in mind? What are the actions? You need to get from goals to an action plan.

You need the Six Steps.

STRUCTURE OF THE SIX STEPS

The Six Steps have three parts and an accompanying website: ***www.sixsteps-goals-action.com***.

A. **Introduction, Strategy Definition, and Organization**
In this section, the foundation is laid to be able to start with the main part: the Six Steps.

B. **The Six Steps**
This is the main part of the book and provides the Six Steps to arrive at the actions.

C. **Conclusion and How to Implement Actions**
In the last section, there is an introduction, "How to Implement Actions," as well as a short résumé of the author and references to those who have helped bring this book to market. This section explains how to find additional information and checklists in the Tools and Techniques Tool Kit on the website, ***www.sixsteps-goals-action.com***.

The next pages will give you a **"Fast A, B, C to Actions."** You will jump over many details and background and can use this page as a guide for your project.

The **"Six Steps"** then start, detailing the background reading (Part A) and all the elements of the Six Steps to Actions (Part B). Finishing your strategic analysis then leads to Step 6: **The Actions Plan, The Strategy**.

STOP, LOOK, AND LISTEN BEFORE YOU JUMP INTO ACTION.

The Six Steps to Action is written as a step-by-step approach. The process is iterative: you will circle back to earlier steps when new information becomes available. The most important part of the strategy process is **observation**. This is presented in Step 3 but, in fact, starts right at the beginning. Make sure that you do spend time registering the first impressions.

Have an **informal round of conversations** with those involved and people that may know about the area you are going to study right at the start. Online you will also find a lot of information. The leading consultancies do publish many reports on the most varied subjects. Read these because these will provide direction to your project and avoid spending a lot of time and effort on something that has been analyzed already.

FAST A, B, C TO ACTIONS

FIRST IMPRESSIONS

Before starting with the Six Steps write down you first impressions, feelings, and observations. Things that seem wrong, those that seem positive, those that strike you in any way.

PART A: INTRODUCTION, STRATEGY DEFINITION AND ORGANIZATION

PART B: 6 STEPS

Step 1. **Area of Analysis** Definition

Step 2. Current Situation **Goals** and Future Situation Goals.

Step 3. **Observations** and **Issues** Generation.

Step 4. **Rank** Issues after Grouping on Immediacy and Impact.

Step 5. Design **Actions**.

Step 6. Agree, Document and **Present**.

PART C: PLAN HOW TO IMPLEMENT ACTIONS

PART A: INTRODUCTION, STRATEGY DEFINITION AND ORGANIZATION **Setting up for Success.**			
Part A. Introduction, Strategy definition and Organization	• Strategy is Action • Get a Team • Stakeholders	>List team members >Engage all impacted by the project	13

PART B: 6 STEPS			
Step 1: Select what you are analyzing.	• What business, organization? • What product/service, market, channel, customer segment, division, country…?	> Write down the area of analysis.	31
Step 2: Set Goals and Objectives in the Present and Future.	• What is the immediate goal? • What is the goal in the future? • What does success look like (End in Mind)?	> Immediate Goal ………. > Future Goal …………… > End in Mind ………….	35
Step 3: Observe and generate issues. *This is the crucial phase, and you need to spend most of your available time on this.*	• What sticks out after a first review (reading, studying a case, listening to customers, looking around, talking to people in ***and outside*** the organization...) • Link the observations to the goals. • Intuitive feeling at the start • Stand back and reflect on what is the key observation.	> List top observations: <u>3 positives:</u> 1. ………………………. 2. ………………………. 3. ………………………. <u>3 negatives:</u> 1. ………………………. 2. ………………………. 3. ………………………. ><u>Key Observation:</u> ……………………….	39
Step 4: Rank Issues.	• The observations go in 2 lists "Current" and "Future" state. For current and future state identify SWOTs. Rank according to impact. • Is there an overriding issue?	> Opportunities > Strengths > Threats > Weaknesses	51
Step 5: Design Actions. **Strategy** is a series of **Actions** to reach **Goals**. In the Present and Future	• 3 <u>actions</u> to stay in place? • 3 <u>actions</u> to reach the future goal?	List current and future goal(s). Identify possible different futures. List actions accordingly and relate to issues.	59
Step 6: Agree, Document and Present	**Summarize**: Issues, barriers and actions to resolve issues. 5 bullet points. Elevator speech ready. Agreement stakeholders. Define what next.	What, who and when on one page (RACI$). Report.	65
PART C. CONCLUSION AND HOW TO IMPLEMENT ACTIONS			
Plan how to implement actions.	Indicate **what, who and when** and an indication of **value**. If you have time do the Six Steps again.	Initial, High-level Strategy	71

PART A

INTRODUCTION, STRATEGY DEFINITION AND ORGANIZATION

PART A: INTRODUCTION, STRATEGY DEFINITION, AND ORGANIZATION

YOUR END IN MIND: AN ACCEPTED ACTION PLAN

You have been asked to prepare a strategy, a plan of action. As a thought experiment, think about a moment where you successfully presented the final, agreed-upon plan.

Imagine the future: imagine your end in mind.

You have just successfully presented a new strategy to the board of your organization. They have seen your Six Steps, leading to an agreed-upon action plan.

Everyone in the room and on Teams was paying full attention after you presented the first slide with the problem definition, key issues, overriding issue, and main action points. And when you mentioned the value the strategy would create, you even had the chairperson fully on board.

You had earlier discussions with all the stakeholders so that everyone in the room was informed about the details, and you had answered all questions and pushbacks in one-on-one conversations.

The participants in the room gave your team a solid go-ahead and were looking forward to being kept up to date with the promised weekly highlights.

The chairperson complimented you and your team on presenting a real plan of action rather than vague objectives, visions, and goals for which attainment cannot be measured.

"Finally, a strategy that is an action plan as it should be. Great that all the actions have clear indicators, and one person is accountable."

Your team enjoyed the celebration and referred to the Six Steps that kept them focused.

Looking back, you are pleased that many misunderstandings that existed in your organization before you started the project have been taken away. The clarification that strategy is a plan of actions was especially useful.

The Six Steps you have used as a manual proved to be very different from other books, written by an experienced practitioner with input from his former team members—and in a few pages, making reading it fast.

Different from many strategies of organizations you studied, you now focus on making goals specific. You have a method to design actions, clearly defined with deliverables that can be measured.

The goals are clear, and you make sure that the first step in the right direction is taken: tackling the barriers to success in the right order.

You and your team look back on a great project with real strategic thinking and an actionable plan as a result.

Let's look back at how you coached your team through the strategy process by going back to the start and, after defining the Strategy is, going through the Six Steps.

Figure 2. Barriers to cross

Example: Distribution and Logistics

Assume that the company you are working for or advising tells you that they "need to improve their distribution."

They tell you they want to build a high-bay automated (robotized) warehouse to reduce costs.

You are asked to "make a strategy to improve distribution."

Based on your experience in strategy projects, you have some concerns because it seems they are jumping right to a solution (the automated warehouse) and don't explain what is wrong with the current distribution, why the solution is the right one even though it may lower costs, etcetera.

There are a series of elements that come before the suggested action can be accepted.

You use the next section to explain this to your client, manager, and your team members.

STRATEGY DEFINITION

To productively collaborate with a team (and leaders) on a strategy (plan of actions), you need to make sure that everyone understands what a strategy is and isn't.

Starting your project, it is good to realize there could be misunderstandings that you need to clarify about strategy. This creates a common language for all involved.

STRATEGY IS:

- ✓ A series of **actions**,
- ✓ developed after thorough **observation** and **analysis**,
- ✓ that will enable a business or organization to reach its **goals** and **objectives**,
- ✓ allowing for the **environment** in which they (will) operate,
- ✓ aligning with all the **stakeholders**,
- ✓ based solidly on the **observations** and deep understanding of the **issues** of the organization.

Strategy and *strategic* are often misused words.

A strategy is a series of **actions** that will enable a business or organization to reach its goals and objectives, allowing for the environment in which they operate and aligning with all their stakeholders. Nothing more, nothing less.

A clear distinction between **goals** and strategy is probably the major difference between organizations that get things done and those that confuse good intentions with making real headway in the direction of the goals.

Goals are related to the **environment** in which the organization operates now and in the future. Understanding those possible environments is part of the process.

From a global perspective (e.g., energy transition), to a smaller scale (e.g., how to adapt to AI in your organization) and personal viewpoint (e.g., how to get your next job), you need action plans that start the work on these issues rather than getting stuck with visions and missions and good intentions that, if there are no results, will lead to endless frustration and even protests.

From time to time, leaders of organizations seem to have only a vague idea where they want to go. If their goals, directions, and required actions are unclear, it is no wonder that their employees are seen as lackadaisical.

There is a need for real strategic thinking and working.

What you will take away from the Six Steps is the understanding that goals, visions, objectives, missions, aspirations, desires, etc. are *not* strategy.

Goals, aims, objectives, vision, mission, purpose, aspirations, and desires are all similar: they are an "end in mind," something to reach in the future. A good "end in mind," however, is clear: it is reached or not.

Without a plan of action, a strategy, these ideas about the future do not have any value. They can be negative because of the demotivating effects on stakeholders when mentioning the future states and never getting there.

Good practice is to define the ends in mind in a way that achievement can be measured. "Being a good place to work" or "contributing to a better world" or "increasing market share" all sound pleasant but have no meaning unless further defined and are not strategic.

Action is important, but a key success factor of a good strategy is not to jump to actions too soon. **Observation**, analysis, and an **understanding of the issues** come first. If you cannot define the problem, you cannot solve it.

Every strategy should create, or avoid losing, **value**. Value touches all aspects of the organization.

Value can be financial or, for a school, the number of students graduating or, for an airport, the waiting time to check in and go through security. Or avoiding losing market share.

Value is the most important measure of success. Value will be defined by the organization and can range from strictly financial shareholder value to measurements including more stakeholders. In the end it is the value for the final customer, in its widest definition, that counts.

A customer can be a consumer buying a product in the supermarket or a client of a lawyer or an applicant for a subsidy at the municipality, etcetera.

Critically analyzing the suggested value is important. Asking why a value indicator is used will lead to more clarity for the strategy development (e.g., Why is the number of students graduating valuable? For whom?).

Make sure that the strategy is always focused on **customer value** creation. Marketing concepts can be used to have the tools and techniques to ensure value delivery, because marketing science is about customer value.

In the strategy process, there will be moments when you get stuck. In that case, go back to the final customer where the real value is created (or lost), and try to make the connection with the observations you made and the issues you are studying.

Figure 3. Defining what is value for the organization in a workshop brings out many issues and ideas around value.

Working back from the end customer means you must interact with the end users, employees, shopkeepers, workshop owners, citizens, etcetera.

In business-to-business value chains, identifying all customers requires more analysis. See Tools and Techniques.

When analyzing customers of products and services, don't forget the internal customers: the stakeholders. These are all the people and parties that can be affected by the strategy and can affect the strategy (goals and actions).

Marketing is not only much broader than selling, it is not a specialized activity at all. It encompasses the entire business. It is the whole business seen from the point of view of the final result, that is, from the customer's point of view.

—*Peter Drucker (1954, 2006)*

This section has given you highlights of what strategy really is. In "Tool and Techniques" on the website, you will find more reading material. "How to Appraise a Strategic Plan" will provide you with another checklist.

CHECKLIST

At the end of each section, there will be a **checklist** to review your project's progress and completeness.

A strategy is a plan of action containing the following elements:

- ☐ A series of **actions**,
- ☐ Creating and protecting **value**,
- ☐ Developed after thorough **observation and analysis**,
- ☐ That will enable a business or organization to reach its **goals and objectives**,
- ☐ Allowing for the **environment** in which they (will) operate,
- ☐ Aligning with all the **stakeholders**,
- ☐ Based solidly on the **observations** and deep understanding of the issues of the organization.

See also "How to Appraise a Strategic Plan" in *www.sixsteps-goals-action.com* section Tools and Techniques.

ORGANIZATION

After reviewing the fundamentals of getting to action plans that form the strategy, you need to get organized for the project.

When you are asked to deliver a strategy or review an existing strategy, there is normally not that much time available. Some simple tools and techniques can be used that enable the team to get to identifying issues and developing solutions quickly while involving all stakeholders.

Depending on the size and complexity of the project, not all steps may be needed. For example, if you plan for an international expansion, you will probably need all the elements, whereas for a case study at university, you will need much less information.

You don't do strategy projects on your own. You need a variety of disciplines (production, legal, human resources, etcetera) to contribute their expertise. You will need these people to provide the connection into their part of the organization.

For example, you will need access to the expertise from HR (human resources) or someone from the HR area on your team. You also need this person to provide the link to HR, someone that knows "who is who" and what is seen as important in HR.

Getting a **team** together and a **formal definition** of the project goes hand in hand.

A system to keep **everyone informed** ("weekly highlights") is recommended.

Before starting the strategy project, make sure that you clearly define the project, you have a team and a client (sponsor), and you update everyone regularly.

"TERMS OF REFERENCE" (TOR)

It is important to have a well-defined project with a clear mandate, budget, and line of reporting. Getting approval for the strategy project is one of the first steps.

You may sometimes decide to start a project without too much involvement from the leaders in your organization. This doesn't necessarily have to be a whistleblowing study but can be something you want to try out on the sidelines. In that case writing the ToR is still a good way to have clarity about your own plan.

The "Terms of Reference" (ToR) detail the problem definition as understood at the start of the project and create clarity on the expected deliverables, budget, and the project organization. It mentions who your client (sponsor) is.

Updates to the ToR will reflect how the problem definition changes over time and ensure that you are not going too far "out of bounds" for your organization. The "highlights" (see later) are a good way to communicate changes in scope and approach.

Don't be too careful when deviating from the ToR: discoveries are not made by staying in the safe harbor.

You will find examples on the website.

Example Stakeholders, Team, and Tools

Working in a company, in politics, or as a student when you are developing a case study, you will get much better results working in a team.

In the distribution example (page 15), you need to consider more than just distribution. Therefore, you are looking for team members from marketing, sales, logistics, finance, etcetera.

You will have a boss, a professor, a business partner, or a client that you need to get on board, and they need to sign off on your plan for the project. This is also the case if they tasked you with the project: when defined more in detail, they may have ideas on how to change the scope. Don't assume they have analyzed all the consequences of launching a study.

Once you have a team and a formal agreement on the project definition (**terms of reference**), it will be important to keep everyone informed of progress (**weekly highlights**).

The team, terms of reference, and weekly highlights together form the **organization** of the project, setting you up for a structured approach to the problem and making sure the members of your team and all stakeholders are aligned.

You will find more details in the next section and examples on the website.

YOUR CLIENT, SPONSOR

Your sponsor can be internal and a member of the leadership team or can be a group of executives or the board of your nonprofit organization. The client can also be external if you work as a consultant.

Because you will bring up observations and issues that are not necessarily welcome, you, as the team leader, or your sponsor will need to be able to remove barriers and limit unnecessary interference.

"Outsiders"

If you are being brought in from outside of an organization to critically observe, analyze, and possibly recommend changes, this is not easy. The challenge is to be independent, not just following instructions, and at the same time, to be "political" enough to "survive" the project.

Being the outsider with a fresh look at things is important. Your client and others will, however, quickly forget that the idea was to get someone "different" in the organization. This is a difficult topic, and many books have been written on this career management aspect. This issue is one of the key reasons why outside advisers and consultants can play a role.

Sometimes you will be a one-man team. Make sure you have someone to bounce ideas off who is bold enough to ask you difficult questions. Train yourself to be your own "devil's advocate." If you cannot explain in a few bullet points (elevator speech) what you have found, you may want to think a bit more before engaging others.

Make sure you have someone senior to ask for advice and direction on a personal basis. This is not always the sponsor of the project but a mentor for yourself, someone you can trust to be objective.

"Insiders"

Many strategy projects are done by people inside the organization.

This is a challenge because the longer you are part of a group, the more you get used to certain ways of looking at things and doing things.

Especially for the analysis part, it will be important to approach outsiders to help the team.

Using outside specialists (customers, distributors, citizens, suppliers, etcetera) helps you to see things differently, and, more important than you may think, they will provide credibility to the project, while you and your team can "hide" behind those specialists. If many customers mention they do not like the service, they can be quoted, and you avoid being the "bad person."

Nevertheless, the messenger of bad news is often somewhat at risk. Make sure you have a senior sponsor on the inside.

This becomes even more important when the project is about yourself, and you are the team (e.g., your career strategy). Having a mentor to keep you "honest" is highly recommended.

If you are the client, make sure that you give space to the team and that they feel free to bring news you may not have expected. Here you can show real leadership.

Realize that all stakeholders will be influenced and change views with every interaction

The Wider Team "Stakeholders"

Influence diagram also in T and T.

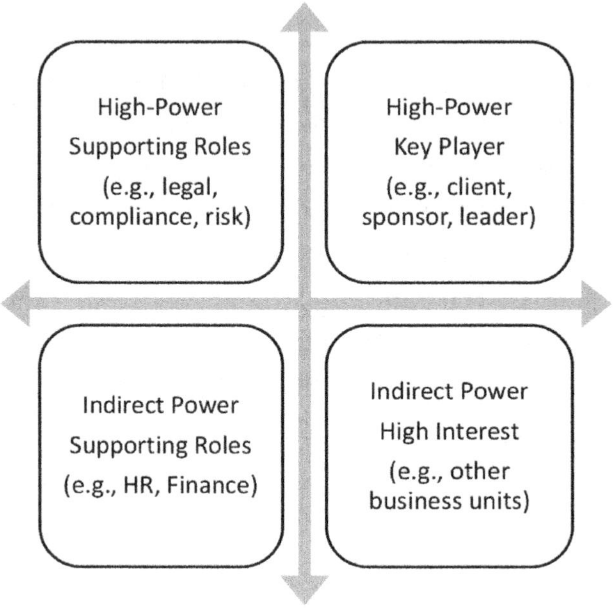

Figure 4. Influence diagram to summarize stakeholders

THE TEAM

Having the Terms of Reference and sponsor defined helps recruiting team members. It is helpful when you have some members of the potential team working together with you on the ToR. That creates buy-in from your team from the start.

Make sure that you have access to the required experience and expertise.

Junior, high-potential team members often are better equipped for a strategy project because they are less used to the way the organization does things. You are looking for critical observers. If you can choose, get a team of high fliers from different departments and backgrounds, both discipline and culture. These will also have less "ballast" and fewer political constraints. Be aware that they may come with special instructions from their superiors or colleagues.

A good team should have a variety of talents: some of your team will be better at designing actions to get issues resolved, whereas others will have special strengths observing, analyzing, and discovering issues. You will need all skill sets, but you will not be successful without the last one.

This is yet another good reason for inclusion and diversity—and a valid reason to engage outside advisers.

Make sure each of your team members is approaching problems differently. Use, for example, MBTI grouping and cultural maps to identify blind spots. See Tools and Techniques.

Most organizations have a strong culture. People in the organization will have a similar profile, and they may have trouble taking a new and different perspective on issues. The culture can be so strong that members of the organization don't realize this themselves.

You need people from different areas in the organization to avoid missing issues and to ensure full buy-in of all the stakeholders.

This has a great advantage for the organization from a people development point of view. Moreover, the experience of the project team stays with the organization and doesn't walk out the door when the project is finished.

As a leader in an organization, you may kick off your own strategy project. You may have identified some areas and issues you want to work on. Define the project and ensure agreement in the organization. Sometimes you want to work on the issues on your own for a while before involving more people.

Once underway, continuously "selling in" (engaging all stakeholders) maintains your support in the organization, and you will know how your stakeholders think about the project's progress. Regular reporting with **weekly highlights** also keeps everyone informed and engaged.

THE WIDER TEAM: STAKEHOLDERS

It is good practice to draw an influence map indicating the process and those involved. These are the so-called stakeholders. They are not on the project team but are crucial to being successful.

Drawing the influence map with a group in front of a whiteboard will ensure that you define the area of strategy completely. An important by-product is that the discussion around the board will give you many ideas about important issues.

Make sure to include all stakeholders who need to sign off on the project. Ask the stakeholders you identified who else may be important for the project.

Some areas tend to be forgotten (e.g., legal and risk). If you want to obtain support after having worked many weeks on the issues and actions, you will have to take them through the whole journey. It is better to involve them right from the start. Keep them posted on progress, and create commitment to bring the project to fruition.

The conversation among the stakeholders about the process and the areas involved will provide many of the key issues as well as indications of solutions. You will get a view on agreement or disagreement among the stakeholders and the dynamics among the players.

You may find that the people in the room are discussing the topic under review for the very first time together and had no idea of the challenges they created for their colleagues further downstream and upstream in the process.

You also may find colleagues that don't function well or knowingly disrupt the process.

WEEKLY HIGHLIGHTS

A good practice is to issue "weekly highlights" from your team reporting to your stakeholders and client/sponsor. These will list key accomplishments as well as providing an early warning for complex issues that may arise in the future. The highlights also enable you to adjust the ToR details as you go along. Depending on the project and the audience, the frequency may be different. Traders will use "daily highlights"; long, stable projects could report monthly.

You want to take your stakeholders with you on the journey and avoid any surprises. Senior leaders don't like surprises. The highlights also serve as a track record of what the team has been working on.

The weekly highlights make sure your team is informed of the overall project, as they may be in different locations and not meet regularly. You will find examples of weekly highlights in Tools and Techniques.

A weekly team call or meeting makes sure that all highlights are mentioned and agreed-upon and potential problems discussed.

With the project now organized, we can get started on the steps to create the strategy. On to Part B: The Six Steps to Actions.

CHECKLIST

The project organization must include the following elements:

- ☐ Terms of Reference
- ☐ The team
- ☐ Client and sponsor
- ☐ Stakeholders identified
- ☐ Weekly highlights

PART B

SIX STEPS TO ACTIONS

1. **Define** the area of analysis.
2. **Set** goals and future situation goals.
3. **Observe** and generate issues.
4. **Rank issues.** Grouping and ranking: immediacy and impact.
5. **Design actions.**
6. **Agree,** document, and present.

And because this is the "Six Steps to Action Manual," there will be more on action in Part C.

PART B: SIX STEPS TO ACTIONS

Six Steps: An Iterative Process

To keep things simple, Six Steps provides a step-by-step plan. This should not be taken as "linear," as it looks at first sight.

The very first thing to do, in fact, is observing, getting a feel for what you are going to work on.

In every step, by taking actions and having interactions with stakeholders, things change. To allow for these changes, you may want to circle back to previous steps to make sure that those changes don't require making adaptions in your process.

No man ever steps in the same river twice, for it's not the same river and he's not the same man. —*Heraclitus, Greek philosopher*

This is a crucial insight. Think about the stakeholders. By interviewing them or having them participate in a workshop, you can get them to start thinking about the issues in ways they may never have. Their ideas mature; they will talk to friends, colleagues, their bosses, etcetera. In a next round, you will have very different conversations.

Think about yourself. You have prepared for your vacation trip; you have read about the destination, and you have spoken to friends who have been there before. Then you go and experience a new country. Your views will have changed. You have spoken with locals: their views on your country will have changed, etcetera.

Make sure you circle back to earlier stages, not in the least because you own views will change as well, and you will observe different aspects of the strategy review.

PART B: THE SIX STEPS

You are now organized. Your team is coming together, you have an agreement summarized in the Terms of Reference, and you have a sponsor. You are ready to start the next phase of your strategy project: making the Six Steps to arrive at your action plan.

Let's go more in detail and explore "the Six Steps":

1. **Define** the **area of analysis**.
2. **Set** current and future **goals**.
3. **Observe** and generate issues.
4. **Rank issues**. Grouping and ranking: immediacy and impact.
5. **Design actions.**
6. **Agree**, document, and present.

Though the steps are presented as a *sequence*, it is crucial to stress again that ***this is an iterative process***. In the first round, Steps 1 and 2 will be rather broad-brush, and these will be fine-tuned in subsequent rounds based on the observations in Step 3.

In fact, every new opportunity for observations can be a "new round" because you are starting to build on earlier observations, and you may see new patterns, and maybe a common theme starts to emerge, something that drives all other observations and issues.

The actions that address the identified issues in the current situation and future situation form the short-term and longer-term strategy.

You will work through the sequence, but keep in mind that this is not a linear program, "ticking the boxes."

Example Area of Analysis

During a production optimization project, you have observed several safety issues, and your focus may change to safety, which means adjusting the terms of reference. You do a round of safety reviews before focusing on production optimization again.

It is also possible that you observe a lack of action resulting from observed safety issues, and that will lead you to questions about the underlying reasons. The question becomes then: What is the "common theme" (culture, tone at the top, lack of training, high staff turnover)?

The area of analysis will become clearer and will change as your team observes more.

Similarly, supplier and customer relations may become clearer, showing a longer supply chain than expected, widening the area of review. Or you discover that a government agency is "duplicated" in different ministries.

This can bring you back to the very first step: "Define the area of analysis."

More examples are on the website analysis in *www.sixsteps-goals-action.com* section Tools and Techniques.

STEP 1: DEFINE THE AREA OF ANALYSIS

DEFINE THE AREA OF ANALYSIS

Though the Terms of Reference (ToR) will define the main purpose and broad area of analysis, it is important to make it very clear what area you are going to analyze.

As we saw in the example on the previous page, the area of analysis can change.

Defining the area is part of the strategy process and will bring up issues to be addressed later.

Getting clarity about the definition of the area under consideration and obtaining agreement from your stakeholders on that definition are important. You don't want to leave things out, and you also want to avoid taking on too much.

The first process step is to define the area of analysis. And even before that, you want to observe, have some first conversations, and do exploratory research.

Once the area is defined, it will also be clear what the adjacent areas are that are influencing your area of analysis or are influenced by your analysis and the strategy that follows. Follow the lead of your observations, expand or reduce the area as you see fit, and document the reasons for the changes. This is then updated in the Terms of Reference to make sure everyone is informed and agrees on the scope change.

There is more on defining the area of analysis in *www.sixsteps-goals-action.com* section Tools and Techniques. "Bain's Adjacencies" provide a checklist on what areas to consider.

Example Area of Analysis: Six P's

A "classical" way to define an area of analysis or segment is using the "Six P's" from marketing theory:

1. Product or services
2. Price or better value
3. Place (distribution, channel, sales)
4. Personnel
5. Promotion (advertising, packaging, etcetera)
6. Presentation

Another way to define the area of analysis is following Abell (1980):

1. Customer groups (categories of customers: <u>Who</u> is satisfied by the service or product?)
2. Customer functions (customer needs: <u>What</u> is being satisfied?)
3. Technologies (<u>How</u> the customer is satisfied?)

Or:

1. Product (the technical product or service)
2. Channel (last step before customer)
3. Brand (image)
4. Price or value

Example Area of Analysis: Distribution and Logistics

For the warehousing example mentioned earlier, it will be important to define what products, pack sizes, serviced customers, kind of transport, etcetera will be the focus of the strategy.

Assume this is a warehouse that only stores and moves full pallets in and out. And every pallet has one type of product/pack. The loading dock at the warehouse is designed for large trailer trucks. Trucks are delivering or taking only full loads.

That would be a very different operation from a warehouse that is set up to distribute pallets loaded with different products or if small vans collect products from the warehouse. When many customers collect products themselves, it becomes an even more fragmented operation.

An indication of what proportion of the business is falling into which category will make clear how the total logistics will be affected. Also, here the intended customers will define the operation.

Example Area of Analysis: Laptops

Making a strategy for "laptops" for a client would be too wide or too high level for a business unit. It would be better to define the analysis narrower (e.g., "Laptops with detachable screens, for the small business segment, bought online with Microsoft software and used for international projects").

STEP 2: SET CURRENT AND FUTURE GOALS

Example: Current Situation and Future Situation Goals

You have been asked to work on the internationalization strategy of a company that has a national monopoly together with two other companies. Internationalization is important because the inclusion of the country into the EU in five years from now will break open the frontiers, and companies from elsewhere can enter the market.

Currently all is quiet, and a lot of cash is generated from the monopolistic market. Everyone has their place, and no inroads are made into one another's areas.

The future goal is clear: international presence to have a more balanced EU portfolio. The future environment is to be explored further.

The current situation goal is important to start with. Maintaining and improving a healthy cash flow to finance international expansion is a clear current goal. If this is not met, the attainment of the future goal becomes difficult.

The current situation has changed already with the news that in five years, the environment will be very different. Colleagues will be starting to work on internationalization, and the operational environment has therefore already changed. Also, companies from abroad will come and start to study opportunities, recruit staff, etcetera.

Obviously, you will need to spend time on the strategy to maintain the current position in the current and changing environment.

"Abroad" is new, and working on the future goal, you will need to reflect on possible future environments for your organization.

STEP 2: SET CURRENT SITUATION GOALS AND FUTURE SITUATION GOALS

In this stage you will look at where the organization is and what it wants to achieve. The first step is that you look at "today" to make sure that the basis from which you start is solid.

Next you will look at the future situation and what the organization wants to be, understanding there may be different possible futures.

You should have some clarity about where to start and where to go. This is more complicated than it seems at first sight. There can be different goals for the short term and long term, and those goals will be in different possible environments (scenarios).

Once there is clarity about the current position and the desired short-term position, you can define the gaps and risks (current issues) based on the observations, and then you can design actions to close those gaps.

Defining the current position will already provide a list of issues.

In general, making plans for the longer-term future without having a robust base to start from is risky.

Only by having clarity on where the organization is does it make sense to start looking at where you want to be.

If you don't know where you want to go, then it doesn't matter which path you take. And this is of course worse when you don't know where you start.

—Lewis Carroll (1865), Alice's Adventures in Wonderland

Next, you need to define the future goal(s). This requires more detail, and you need to know why those goals have been defined and *what future circumstances have been assumed.*

Goals and objectives should be measurable.

Goals are not actions. From time to time, you will see statements like: "We will improve our market share" or "We will become more inclusive." Those are not goals because they have no clear, measurable point of achievement.

A goal is either reached or not reached or maybe partially reached but always needs to be clearly quantifiable.

"In 2030 our market share will be more than 25 percent" and "50 percent or more of our board members in 2025 will be female" are clear and measurable, and therefore strategic, goals.

As mentioned earlier, clarity around goals and strategy (actions) distinguishes organizations that "get things done" from those with good intentions.

An example is many governments' "strategy" for energy transition; there are many goals but no strategy. Having no clear goals means that no clear actions can be defined to make or measure progress.

For example, the goal to have "all cars electric by 2030" overlooks the barriers of not enough loading stations and not enough electricity transport capacity.

A key tool to avoid your organization falling in the "mission/vision" trap is to have a clear definition of the barriers and hurdles to cross to meet the "end in mind," as explained by Covey (1997).

Example: Current Situation and Future Situation Goals 2

A public media company for which privacy rules are going to change will need to implement a set of actions (compliance strategy) to remain viable as a business. Defending the current position ("A").

If the public media company aspires to grow by capturing market share from others, another set of actions (growth strategy under new compliance rules) will be required to reach that target ("B").

The "A" is from the recommended book on leadership and strategy, From A to B (Van der Veer, 2023).

Jalaja Ahuja (master student at Erasmus) defined "Beyond B" because there are often multiple possible futures and even completely different possible views on the future as well as "stretch goals."

Figure 5. Jalaja presenting "Beyond B"

The definition of goals is one of the strategy elements dependent on the analysis in the subsequent steps.

Further study may change the definition of the area under review and provide more clarity on the organization's strengths and weaknesses.

This then enables you to either validate the goals or change these.

If the analysis shows that the market is smaller than you previously assumed, the current market share is in fact higher, and the future market share goal may need to be adjusted.

If, on the other side, the analyses show that the market conditions are going to be much more difficult than expected, the growth aspirations may have to be adjusted downward.

In situations with high uncertainty in the future (or in the immediate present), it is advisable to define "alternative future" scenarios and repeat the issue generation, ranking, and actions steps (a "sensitivity analysis").

For more details on Covey's end-in-mind method, scenario planning, and sensitivity analysis, see *www.sixsteps-goals-action.com* section Tools and Techniques.

CHECKLIST

For current and future goals:

- ☐ Current environment (status quo) > goals
- ☐ Changes in the current environment > goals 2
- ☐ Future environment > goals 3
- ☐ Alternative future environment (scenarios) > goals 4
- ☐ Unexpected future environment (scenarios) and stretch goals > goals 5

STEP 3: OBSERVE AND GENERATE ISSUES

Example Observation Warehouse

Your team is tasked to study the spare parts for Mercedes trucks for the Benelux and define "design parameters for a high-bay automated warehouse" "like they have in Spain." Note that the solution is already given in the project definition. Always be watchful when that happens and don't assume this is based on robust research or study. Jumping to action will lead you and your team to wrong conclusions.

After getting a team together, your first step will be to visit the planned location, then to the manufacturing plant on one of Europe's largest industrial estates.

Checking in and getting permits to drive to the factory will provide you with a first observation. Would it make sense to build a warehouse for packaged goods in the middle of such a facility? How would this work with trucks driving onto the loading zone?

Your team interviews many people, mostly one on one and in their areas of work, to get an independent view and understand the context of the answers and observations. Next, you visit a high-bay automated warehouse to see how it looks and operates. Obviously, this is for high rotation streams of goods with full pallets going in and out. The operators explained that order collection of less-than-full pallets wasn't efficient for this kind of warehouse. Distributors and dealers collecting products in different types of vans and trucks is something that the company finds very important to keep distributors loyal and dealers connected with the experts. You find that their vans and cars added complexity and were not allowed at the loading docks of that warehouse.

Your team noted that the visited warehouse was operated by a third-party operator that also carried out distribution to final customers.

To make a long story short: After meeting logistics specialists from outside the company and getting indications of operating costs, you and your team have decided to change the study to third-party, off-site logistics as an alternative for cheaper and safer operations, and higher customer service levels.

STEP 3: OBSERVE AND GENERATE ISSUES

In this phase it is all about going out and observing, talking with people, asking for views, and listing what you find.

You want to start early, and you may even do some informal interviews before writing up the Terms of Reference. Often, a few are enough to start formulating some hypotheses on the key issues and what the real problem may be.

Don't assume anything; you'll make an ass of u and me. —*Oscar Wilde*

Observation is the key challenge when creating a strategy.

In the end problem-solving (and keeping strengths) is, of course, what you are hired for, but this comes after finding issues (problems and strengths) by observing.

"Issues" are not only "problems" but also aspects that are strengths, or other elements that stand out as special, different, unexpected, etcetera.

Observations are subjective and based on the observer's background, experience, and training. Another reason to have diverse and inclusive teams and to have each team member observe independently without "pushing" them in a certain direction.

Observation is the active acquisition of information. This can be seeing, listening, reading, participating, reviewing reports, interviewing people, etcetera.

Observations can be grouped into areas, and the issues that follow from the observations can be developed.

Once observations are grouped and ranked for importance, you can start looking at the issues related to the observations and test these further. You can also look for "common themes."

It is important to stress again that observing will lead to positive as well as negative issues. You may observe an error in a spreadsheet as well as the very organized office space and relaxed atmosphere.

As a team leader, you may want to ask for those positive issues because most people tend to go "negative" also, depending on their cultural background. Start with positive and end with negative. This is like Learning Points, as explained in in *www.sixsteps-goals-action.com* section Tools and Techniques.

Figure 6. Observing is a skill that can be learned.
Do you see the key issue in this picture? Solution in T and T.

The very first impression often hints at relevant differentiators or issues. It is good practice to ask team members to write down their observations before starting to share these, to avoid influencing each other.

A good practice is to have everyone write these on Post-its, collect these, and put these on a whiteboard or wall. This helps avoid observations being held back when team members or others listen to their colleagues.

If you are the only observer, make sure you write down your first impressions immediately, as these are very "perishable goods."

You can compare this phase with the diagnosis of a doctor.

The next step of the diagnosis is the understanding of the observations and looking deeper to find underlying meaning and reasons and formulate key issues by asking "why" and using, for example, the Pyramid Principle (Minto 2009) to look for reasons (drivers) of the issues and observations.

There are checklists and frameworks to help generate and categorize issues in the T and T Tool Kit on the website. It requires observing and trying to understand more by asking questions (five times "Why?") and looking in different ways and different timeframes and through different analytical "glasses": financial, organizational, branding, legal, shareholders, inside and outside stakeholders, etcetera.

Sometimes observations are not easy to pin down. Feelings and intuition are valid at this phase; make sure these are documented to be able to analyze these later. Don't underestimate the vague feeling one may have about an area of observation.

Observations can be improved in reach and depth by using checklists to see whether these trigger different observations.

For example, if you are asked to look for fire hazards, you will find other things than if you are asked to investigate access security. If you are preconditioned by being asked to look for failures, you may not see the successes.

Good observations and identifying issues are the key and first steps to creating a strategy. This is where analytical power and curiosity play a key role.

Regularly step back and reflect on what the top "key issue" is. What comes up as *the* most important strength, challenge, barrier, problem? If you don't do this, you may do a lot of work to define actions that may resolve minor issues but find that these cannot be implemented because of this overriding main barrier—for example, studying how to drive to a destination without having a driving license or arguing about who pays for the tickets for the grandchildren when you find out that they don't have valid passports.

From time to time, it is better to go back to the observation and diagnosis phase and look at things again, with a new set of hypotheses to test.

Observing and generating issues is the most important part of the strategy process. It is a challenging phase because we must continuously remind ourselves not to jump to any conclusions and especially not to go into action mode. It also requires practice and having people on your team that have high levels of analytical skills. Ask questions, don't discard issues, try to understand what team members bring up, and trust their feelings.

A good habit is to write down five key issues every day with your team and review these daily. Don't make any assumptions. Try to understand, and don't argue whether an issue is valid or not at this stage. This focuses the team and keeps your sponsor informed. Keep an open mind, as the discussion of the key issues and the topics brought to the table can all potentially change the direction of your project.

As mentioned, **the very first step of a strategic analysis is to inventory all the information that may be relevant**. From studying that information, observations, issues, and barriers will emerge.

Very often you will need to read extensive presentations and reports to discover or formulate possible issues and barriers. Save yourself a lot of time by making a good list of sources you are using and the observations from those sources.

Document who mentioned what to be able to go back for clarification or to use as sources.

Potential initial observation sources are reports and the internet:

a. Profit and loss accounts
b. Annual reports
c. Market research
d. EIU reports on countries and industries
e. Sector reports
f. Chambers of commerce
g. *Financial Times* and similar
h. Searching the internet

Pay special attention to the CEO's speeches and write-ups for the annual report. Senior leaders will repeat themes they find important. Try to understand how these points relate to your analysis.

It is then good practice to get your team together to brainstorm based on observations (be careful to park any suggestions for solutions or actions, and don't discard what seems unimportant right now). Talking together about what each team member has read, heard, and observed will generate new insights and ideas and many questions. Write these down. There will be a team member whose strength is documenting observations and discussions.

Scribbr.com provides easy-to-use source generators for news articles and books.

Mind-mapping tools can be helpful to write everything down and order later.

If this is a university/school business case that you are asked to analyze, read the case description and search for additional information if needed. Then step back ("raise the helicopter" to get an overview) and write down the key points that come to mind.

A good practice is to summarize "what is going on" in five short bullet points.

The next step is interacting with people inside and outside the organization. You will find that some informal conversations about the topic, both in and outside the organization, will help focusing on the important areas. But keep an open mind.

a. Interviews

In a real-life situation, you want to engage people inside and outside the organization at different levels. Only do this when you have prepared yourself and your team with the information available. You want to have meaningful, in-depth interviews rather than going through a list of questions or, worse, asking questions you could have found the answers to easily.

Use the fact that you are new to the subject and are supposed to be "ignorant" to ask people in the organization for their views.

People in the middle of events often know less about them than those watching from the outside, which is why interviews with senior business figures inform us about what these people think rather than what is happening.

So when someone tells you something is too complex for you to understand, the usual reason is that they do not really understand it themselves. Sometimes they know that they do not really understand it: often they do not.

—Sir John Kay, one of Britain's leading economists and author of The Hare & the Tortoise: An Informal Guide to Business Strategy (www.johnkay.com)

Use interview techniques as explained in T and T, and listen to interviews by reporters to train yourself and your team to have these conversations.

The key point is "to not lead the witness."

Get your team together again to write down and discuss all the issues that were mentioned (be careful to park any suggestions for solutions or actions). You will also get new insights from your team.

b. Site visits

Go where the action is: a factory, a warehouse, the waiting room of the municipality, the street corner opposite a shop, etcetera. Use common sense in public spaces, and either make yourself known or ask permission. You are a strategy analyst, not a secret service agent.

c. Customer interviews

With that information you can go "outside" and see the reality as presented by customers and maybe competitors. The channel participants (retailers, distributors) and the wider value chain (suppliers) will also be valuable sources of information to generate issues.

A great way to get direct and indirect exposure to customer issues is to join salespeople and delivery staff in their daily activities. The CEO of Coolblue regularly takes the place of one of the people on the delivery truck. By helping with the delivery of goods, he gets to listen to real customers, and by sharing a day in the truck, he gets to hear from the driver about what else is going on.

These are the most important sources of information and, in fact, the easiest to use to discover issues when you listen well and remind yourself to ask open-ended questions.

You and your team can then review how the "inside" and "outside" observations compare.

d. Be the customer

Experience how it is to be a customer. Call your help-desk number. Try the website, go buy a raincoat, apply for a driving license, etcetera. This could be the topic of a book. Going out and experiencing what your target group sees and feels is one of the best inputs for an action plan. See T and T for some examples.

e. Expert groups

With background information and certain hypotheses, one can organize a workshop with people who have direct and indirect experience of the area. As the background information is presented, observations and issues will be mentioned and can be listed, grouped, and ranked.

f. External expert groups

The same can be done with clients, industry experts, etcetera

Issue generation when discussing key success factor ranking is a good tool to use. This also links observations to the next step: issues grouping and ranking.

You can also ask outsiders to visit your operations. But not just for fun! Ask them to observe and mention three things to you after the visit they found remarkable or surprising, things they did not expect before the visit.

However, if they think they see something unsafe, ask them to mention this immediately. They may observe a dangerous situation that others don't see anymore because they have gotten used to it.

The output of this Step 3 is a list of observations and issues; these need to be grouped and ranked for importance in Step 4.

CHECKLIST

Check all possible sources:

- ☐ Reports and internet searches
- ☐ Interviews
- ☐ Site visits
- ☐ Customer interactions
- ☐ Be the customer
- ☐ Expert groups
- ☐ Initial observations/feelings
- ☐ Daily team review

Example 1: Where are the gas stations?

Figure 7. Where?

A national oil company wanted to start building business abroad. They bought a series of gas stations. On paper it looked good. The newly hired manager with more international experience pushed back and suggested an on-site review of the gas stations to be acquired. The investment bankers were not pleased, but a team was sent abroad with the list of stations.

After the sixth call from the "middle of nowhere," when the team stated they didn't find anything but the dilapidated remnants of what had been gas stations, the due diligence process was extended from just paperwork to a full site inventory.

As they say in the Netherlands: "The truth is in the street."

Go out and see reality.

Example 2: Why do the large packs of milk not sell?

Figure 8. Too much of a good thing?

A dairy company had introduced two-liter containers for milk. Consumer research had indicated interest for larger packs. The leader of the team working on packaging was in the supermarket and decided to hang back and observe (after introducing himself to the supermarket manager).

Quickly, he noted that lifting the packs from the fridge bottom into the shopping trolley was too heavy for most clients, who preferred the easy-to-handle one-liter packs, something you only learn when leaving the office and observing.

Go out and see reality.

Example 3: Observations can be made in the office as well.

A deal team was involved in a series of acquisitions of bottled gas businesses. To calculate the long-term profitability and the amount the company was willing to pay, an elaborate spreadsheet was developed by head office with input from technicians and experts and signed off by the leadership team. The young analyst on the team managed the spreadsheet and provided the deal leader with the target acquisition amount based on working capital and discounted future cashflows.

One day the analyst and deal leader ended up ahead of the team in Rio de Janeiro, and after seeing the sights, they got a meeting room in the hotel to get some work done.

The analyst used the large screen to review inputs on the spreadsheet. The deal leader looked up at the screen and was impressed by the details. He knew from earlier work that a large component of the working capital was the number of bottles in circulation and asked the analyst what number he used. He said: "Glad you asked. Actually, when making the spreadsheet, I had no clue and didn't think this important. I just put a number in to make the calculations work." The number he put in was two per customer: "One bottle at the customer and one in the factory being filled."

From earlier projects, the deal leader remembered that the number of bottles is more than four: one to two at the customer's house (depending on the country), one in transport, one full in the warehouse, one on the production line, and one to two empty in the warehouse and the repair shop. In total around six, a factor of three more and representing a major part of the working capital.

The analyst was a bit embarrassed, and he said that no senior executive ever took the time to look at the details in the spreadsheet with him. It was also not a culture where a junior analyst would ask a senior manager for input. The team had made several acquisitions and now understood why their price offered was accepted with such big smiles by the sellers.

Take time as a leader with your team members individually to look at what everyone is doing and what issues may be hidden in extensive spreadsheets and calculations. Ask what the key issues are in their work. More examples on the website.

STEP 4: RANK ISSUES AFTER GROUPING ON IMMEDIACY AND IMPACT

Example of Good Key Issue Practice

You will discover that remembering issues and keeping everyone focused on the key issues at every stage of the project is a challenge.

One of the team leaders of ABS (Analysis and Business Strategy) used an effective method to keep everyone on the team focused on the key issues at various stages in the project.

Every evening before going to dinner, he would ask the team for the five key issues and the five key barriers to success.

That would postpone dinner, as it sometimes took some arguing before the team agreed. The discussion was, of course, very useful, and notes were made to remember the things that came up, especially disagreements and concerns.

The team leader would write the five top issues on the back of the blackboard. The next morning, the issues would be reviewed and confirmed or adjusted. It was interesting to write these down daily and see how these developed over the course of a project as ideas changed, and the team found new information.

Figure 9.

During the project you will continuously group the observations and issues. Observations are what you see ("Shopper cannot lift a heavy two-liter pack from the shelf"); the issues and barriers to success are "Are packing sizes right for easy handling?" or "Are large packs in the right place?" (Beer crates are also heavy...but not cooled.)

You now have lists of observations, notes of meetings, highlighted parts in documents, etcetera.

These need to be listed and organized around themes. A group exercise with Post-its on a wall works well. Take notes on the emerging issues. Explaining the results to the stakeholders is a good way to have a conversation about the observations.

Frameworks can be used to structure the results of these categorizing exercises (McKinsey's 7-S structure, BCG matrix, Porter's Five Forces).

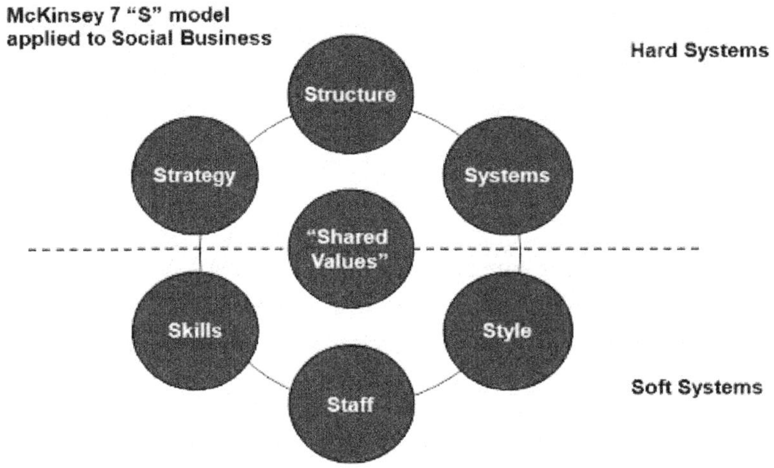

Figure 10. McKinsey 7 "S" Model

Resolving conflicting issues is done by raising a new issue. For example, some claim a growing market share. Others mention the issue of a declining market share, and others question the definition of the area under review. The new issue and barrier to success is: "There is no consensus about the market share development (or definition) of the (maybe not well-defined) area under consideration."

This is a good observation and could be classified either under "shared values" or "systems" in the McKinsey 7-S model.

Dividing issues into internal (strengths and weaknesses) and external (opportunities and threats), current and future, is another way to organize the findings and, like the other categorizing tools, also serves as a list to trigger issues you may have missed.

The next step is placing the observations in groups and ranking these according to importance.

It is crucial to stand back and reflect on the key issues that affect the current situation because these will require the most attention.

Sometimes one key issue may override all others. This may be an issue that, if not resolved, makes the current position untenable and, if those issues are not resolved, turns future goals into purely hypothetical ones. Don't discuss the location of deck chairs on the *Titanic*: making a marketing plan for a company that is about to go under doesn't make sense.

Ranking the observations according to value to the organization and complexity of resolving (impact and effort) is another clear way to summarize the analytical phase.

The process of ranking the observations and issues with the people responsible for the implementation is important to deliver value for the organization.

FIND THE "COMMON THEME."

After grouping the observations and organizing these into key issues, the next challenge is to find a common theme, the overriding issue.

This requires looking at the analysis from a higher level. Actions that address those main barriers or defend a hidden strength of the organization create real value.

> ***In meetings of strategic importance, do you articulate the bigger-picture narrative? If not, remember to "elevate your perspective to help shape the context in which details can then be explored."***
>
> *—Brenda Steinberg and Michael D. Watkins, from IMD "10 Ways to Prove You're a Strategic Thinker"*

For example, you may find several issues around pricing, losing customers, unexpected complaints, etcetera. The common theme is a lack of customer intimacy. That needs to be addressed, and the individual points for improvement need to be aligned. Other issues, though important, may have a lower ranking when not fitting into the common theme group.

Another example is when people protest a policy, but the common theme is that they don't feel heard rather than disagreeing with the specific policy.

Figure 11. Team brainstorming and categorizing issues
Example of whiteboard exercise where the observations and issues have been grouped.

Meghan Fisher is listening to comments from the group (about 30 people of a business division) after the first day to make sure nothing is missing. Kathlyn de Cardenas is making notes to enable later follow-up. The process is guided by the author Maarten J.L. van Hasselt.

RANK ISSUES

As mentioned, the major risk in strategy creation is jumping to solutions. Designing and implementing actions before observing carefully is often not productive. A full inventory and analysis of *all* the issues and barriers must come first, in the current and future environments, across the organization.

Make sure you get this right.

> ***Analysis is the critical starting point of strategic thinking.*** —*Ohmae (1982)*

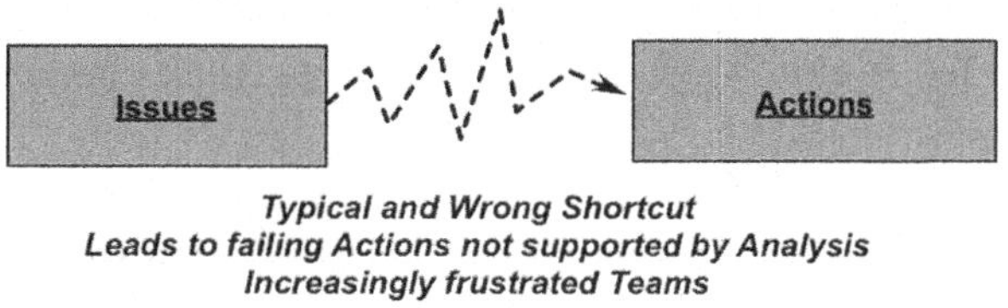

Figure 12. Ohmae, Typical shortcut: Too soon to actions

"Doing something" feels good. There may be a lot of pressure to show action. From time to time, your and other people's actions distract from—and even lead away from—making the business or organization stronger and reaching its goals.

Make sure that all observations have been considered and explained. Assess all the barriers, clearly formulating the underlying strengths or problems. If you don't have a clear problem, you cannot resolve it. Not knowing *why* your current position is strong, you cannot keep doing the right things.

Think before you act.

If I had an hour to solve a problem, I'd spend 55 minutes thinking about the problem and five minutes thinking about solutions.—*Einstein*

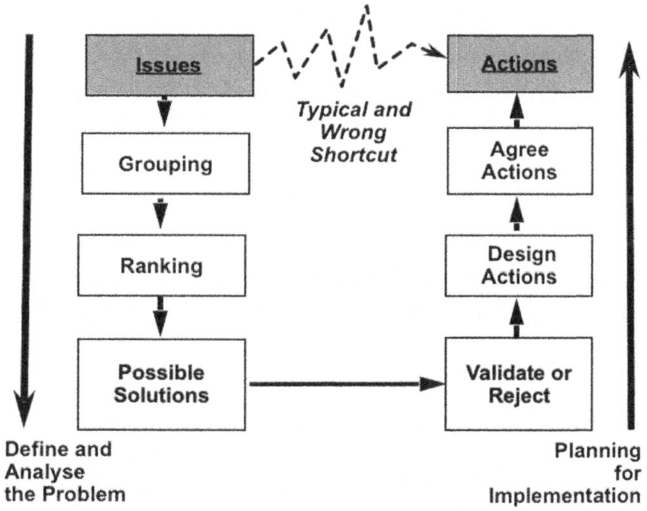

Figure 13. Ohmae, Robust process from issues to actions

See this as a **diagnosis of a business or organization**. Don't focus on the problems only, and give sufficient time and space to positive observations. Acknowledge the things that go well, as these are a foundation from which you work on change and motivate the people working in the organization and other stakeholders.

Be aware that organizations "self-diagnose" and may push you to action ("Make a web-based promotion plan" or "Have smaller classes"). Like a good general practitioner, you should never accept the patient's self-diagnosis.

When you are running an organization, day-to-day activities and decisions make it quite challenging to step back and reevaluate your strategy. This is one of the (few) reasons why outside advisers may help you. They take a distant view to observe those things you are so used to and don't see anymore.

...They ask questions and don't let go. And they're incredibly curious: our young talents' most important quality. They will shape the changes, growth, and successes of your organization together with you. —*Ormit Talent website*

In many cases the problems, and the strengths, of the organization are not clearly recognized. This occurs because insiders don't have an analytical overview. Bringing up issues is not always welcomed by the leadership ("No, Mr. President, you are wrong!"). From time to time, recognizing issues can be seen as a personal failure.

It is very important to stress the strong points. Those are the ones the organization can build on. These often enable its continued existence and open possibilities to improve further. Sometimes, more often than we think, not enough emphasis is given to this. From time to time, we may conclude that things are good as they are, and no action is required to reach the goals.

"Don't change a winning team!"

And make sure that the winning team gets as much support, attention, budget, etcetera, as the struggling team. Bringing a 7/10 to 9/10 may have a bigger impact than bringing a 5/10 to a 6/10.

It requires standing back, taking some distance to see "the obvious."

An insider is like a fish in a fishbowl, unable to see the exact shape of its surroundings even though those surroundings are perfectly clear to everyone else.

—*Xu Zhiyuan (2015) as quoted in Baggini (2019)*

"Sequence," sticking to the right order even under pressure and looking at the big picture as well as at the details ("helicopter quality") while stepping back from the immediate pressures, is a crucial success factor for strategic thinking.

CHECKLIST

- ☐ List all issues
- ☐ Group in categories
- ☐ Immediacy (now or later)
- ☐ Impact on the value (high or low)
- ☐ Brainstorm
- ☐ Look at old list of issues
- ☐ Initial observations/feelings
- ☐ Overriding Issue
- ☐ Common theme
- ☐ Diagnose no actions
- ☐ Mention all the strong points
- ☐ Use different points of view

Figure 14

STEP 5: DESIGN ACTIONS

You are now getting to "actions." Make sure that the previous phases are complete. Actions must be supported by the analysis in the previous four steps.

Designing actions to resolve issues and to remove barriers enable the organization to reach its goals.

You have ranked the Issues (positive and negative) that form the barriers you need to overcome to reach the goals, under different scenarios.

The actions to overcome those barriers, in the right sequence, and prioritizing those actions to avoid "sliding backward" are the strategy.

Being very careful and complete with your observations enables you to define actions that bring you closer to the end in mind, rather than talking about how lofty and fantastic the end in mind is.

Your strategic actions are going to address these key issues, removing the barriers to reach the end in mind.

The priorities are determined by the value at risk (current situation) and the value to be gained (future situation). Don't forget actions to keep the strong points.

From "the Six Steps," we have now completed 1–4, and we are working on Step 5:

1. **Define** *the area of analysis.*
2. **Set** *current and future goals.*
3. **Observe** *and generate issues.*
4. **Rank issues**. *Grouping and ranking: immediacy and impact.*
5. <u>**Design actions**</u>.
6. **Agree**, *document, and present.*

Summarizing with an example:

Step:	Example:
You have **listed observations** from **Step 3**, on the area of customer service from **Step 1**.	"Long waiting times for help-desk calls"; "Unhappy clients"; "Stressed-out staff"
From those observations you have made **lists of Issues ranked** according to when these may occur (immediacy) and how much impact (value) **Step 4**.	"How to improve waiting time for help-desk calls" to reach the level of client service as determined as a **goal in Step 2** and reducing staff turnover, lowering stress.
For those issues, you **design actions, Step 6**.	"Have more help-desk staff"; "How to attract more staff"; "How to make the job more attractive"; etcetera

In the example you may also want to step back and think about a **higher-level issue**: "Why are there so many calls?" "Is there a quality issue that leads to this?" And in that case, the action may be completely different. Go back to asking "Why?" five times and Minto's Pyramid Principle.

See an example in *www.sixsteps-goals-action.com* section Tools and Techniques how to use Ohmae's concepts (Figure 13) and the key issues process to get from key success factors ranking to key issues and actions.

Example Designing Actions: Safety

You have observed several safety issues working on a production optimization strategy.

Your focus will have changed to safety.

You observe a lack of action resulting from observed safety issues.

The question becomes then: What is the "common theme"—culture, tone at the top, lack of training, high staff turnover?

You find it is high staff turnover.

The actions needed to have a safe production will then focus on how to keep people in the organization while making sure that onboarding instills the right safety awareness.

Reducing the safety incidents has been the right action to take a major barrier away for production optimization.

Use the following categories for the strategic action plan based on the observations and issues:

a. **Actions to maintain the current state.**

   This is not necessarily "standing still" or "avoiding slipping backward" but could be maintaining current growth or improvement levels. For example, sales have been increasing by 5 percent per year, and these actions make sure that this growth rate is maintained.

b. **Actions to improve or grow further.**

   This is the set of actions that will remove barriers to make progress toward the longer-term goal. For example, actions required to increase growth to 10 percent per year, increasing market share, becoming part of the global leading group, etcetera.

c. **Actions to make a step change.**

   These are the actions that move performance, sales, inclusiveness, safety, etcetera, to a much higher level. This could be a paradigm shift for the organization. This often requires actions that investigate and determine the nature of barriers to move to that next level. It would mean moving to a market leadership position, becoming the best-in-class in quality performance, an example in inclusiveness, etcetera.

As mentioned in the first chapter, everyone loves to get into action. Now you need to be very critical so that the actions are indeed linked to the most important issues and barriers. Sequence and cost/value evaluations are important at this stage.

Analyzing the issues and designing actions to cross those barriers will show the relations between them. The art is to see the cause-and-effect relationships and which action needs to come first.

Keep searching for overlooked issues that may "overrule" all other issues and options. These can be new or existing barriers that need to be addressed before moving on to the end-in-mind goals. These are often financial (the business is making heavy losses, and paying for improvement options is questionable), the organization will get new leadership, the product or service becomes obsolete, there are sudden changes in the environment, etcetera.

Actions or deliverables need a very concise definition to be able to determine when they are completed or how far implementation has progressed. "Increasing market share" is not an action but an objective that will have actions related to it and needs to be quantified.

The challenge in this phase is to be very specific. Make the actions **SMART$**:

- **S**pecific
- **M**easurable
- **A**chievable
- **R**elevant
- **T**ime-bound
- **$**: Quantifying the value resulting from the action

Assign **r**esponsibility and **a**ccountability clearly. Agree on who needs to be **c**onsulted and **i**nformed. **RACI**:

- **R**esponsible
- **A**ccountable
- **C**onsult
- **I**nform

Examples are in *www.sixsteps-goals-action.com* section Tools and Techniques.

Plan and make sure that you are realistic about available capacity. Often, team members and members of leadership are scheduled for much more time than they have available.

The measure of success is protected value or future value created. This can often be done in monetary terms. Make sure that a clear measure is agreed upon that is not open for debate.

Watch for general statements like "improving membership value"; be precise to enable measurement of progress to avoid "excuses."

These values can be listed under a generic goal but individually need to be clear. Defining the value parameters often leads to discussion that indicates that a full consensus may not have been reached.

"Increasing market share" is too vague, and it is better to have a concise goal (e.g., increasing market share from 14 percent to 22 percent by the end of 2025).

Market share needs to be defined clearly:

> The business school's market share will be defined as the number of certified bachelor's degrees for the international MBA program of RSM divided by the number of same degree of all business schools that participate in the OneMBA program, on September 1 of every calendar year, starting in 2024.

It is helpful to have a group session to challenge the definition to be able to land on a watertight number. The legal expert may be able to help tighten this up a bit more.

Examples and further explanation of RACI, SMART$, Traffic Lights, etcetera, are found on the website.

CHECKLIST

Check you have all the actions documented clearly:

- ☐ Actions to maintain current state
- ☐ Actions to improve or grow further
- ☐ Actions to make a step change.
- ☐ RACI
- ☐ SMART$
- ☐ Do actions address all issues/barriers
- ☐ Have actions been agreed upon and assigned?

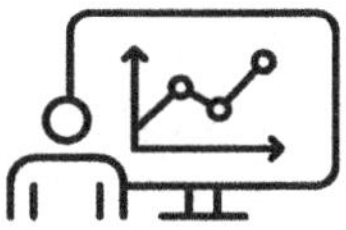

STEP 6: AGREE, DOCUMENT, AND PRESENT

Example: Agreement and Presentation

You can go back to the Terms of Reference (ToR) and make sure that all elements have been dealt with. The weekly highlights will remind you of the things you and your team did. Meeting the stakeholders to sell-in the conclusions is important before making the final presentation and sending out the reports.

If you do all the steps to perfection, you will present on the first slide the problem, solution, and value. The CEO or COO of the client will get up and say: "I agree, good plan. Get going."

Some people think that they need to show all the things they did, including the dead ends they pursued, to get to the conclusion, as if to justify the time they spend on the project.

You know that is not the case.

If the leadership wants to know the journey, they will ask, but like children in the back of your car, they are only interested in getting to the destination: value for the CEO, the pancake house for the kids...

Value is not increased by showing that it took you a lot of work to get there.

It is very tempting, but you have seen that it really positions you and your team well when "cutting to the chase": after all, you have sent regular updates of your activities through the weekly highlights, and everyone knows the road you took.

More examples are on the website.

You want to make sure that all the issues and resulting actions are documented and presented. You need to get the agreement of the stakeholders that this is the way to go.

Documenting the strategy is rather straightforward after the work done so far. The format depends on your organization.

Document keeping the audience in mind, often senior leadership. It is very important to remind yourself that they want to see the value created right up front.

If you present to leaders and members of the organization you have reviewed, don't forget that they know the organization quite well. That means you can skip explaining that and jump straight into the real added value of your work. The structure suggested is "**P S I V A**":

- **P**roblem definition, including value at risk
- **S**olution and cost benefit summary
- **I**ssues: "Proof" of issues addressed
- **V**alue: "Proof" of value created
- **A**ction plan (RACI or similar)

SELLING IN

One of the reasons the final presentation can be short and to the point is that following the process of Six Steps, you will have spent quite some time "selling in" the project to all the stakeholders throughout the process.

SIGN OFF

At this stage, it is good to go back to the updated version of the Terms of Reference (ToR) to check that you have indeed achieved the objectives of the project. The final weekly highlights (as far as this specific project is concerned) can mention that the project has been concluded and the actions have been agreed upon and signed off.

Though this seems a bit formal, it is worthwhile to give everyone the good news and to formally document that senior leadership, your client, your boss, the minister, your team, and stakeholders have received the report out and have agreed to the analysis and action plan. If unavoidable, you can document which points of disagreement still exist. These can be worked out during the implementation. Don't ignore these!

COMMUNICATE AND UPDATE

As mentioned, after sign-off and approval of the strategy project, the work of implementation starts.

It is important to remain visible for the leadership and stakeholders and not wait to be asked to report on progress. Be proactive; start new highlights reporting on progress as well as encountered problems or issues that you think may come up in the future. Most leaders don't like surprises. Show you are in control by also mentioning the things that are "out of control."

Because change is the only constant, it is important to keep monitoring all the factors that influence the agreed-upon strategy and when necessary, adapt or, in some instances, even redo the project. Make sure you keep informing the stakeholders, and keep the communication channels open in both directions.

CHECKLIST

Elements for reporting out and documenting:

- ☐ Refer back to Terms of Reference
- ☐ Check highlights
- ☐ Short and conclusion up front
- ☐ "P S I V A" structure
- ☐ Selling in completed before presenting
- ☐ Sign-off documented
- ☐ Communicate and updates
- ☐ Hand over to implementation team
- ☐ Start new highlights series
- ☐ Are all influencing factors unchanged?

PART C

CONCLUSION AND HOW TO IMPLEMENT ACTIONS

CONCLUSION AND HOW TO IMPLEMENT ACTIONS

Now the next phase starts: **implementing the agreed-upon actions** and keeping sponsors, team members, and stakeholders informed.

As mentioned, you don't want to jump to actions, but once you have an agreed-upon strategy with clear actions, it is obvious that nothing changes without implementation.

That area will be described briefly and may be the topic for a next book, from getting to an action plan to implemented actions.

Depending on your organization and whether you are an inside or outside project leader, the roles now change.

From program lead, the responsibility now moves to the implementation lead. When you are a member of the organization, it makes sense to be made responsible for the implementation.

There is a caveat. A project leader may become too careful, not stretching the objectives, knowing that they will be responsible for the delivery of the plan.

The profile of the leader of the strategy project is often more analytical.

In all cases the top role now changes from strategy project leader to implementation or delivery/change leader.

Once the actions have been taken to enable the implementation of the strategy, there may be a next change from delivery/change leader to organization leader. That will happen when all changes have been implemented and the new steady state needs to be managed.

An example is an internationalization project where, after the acceptance of the strategy action plan made by the strategy project leader, the business development leader establishes distributors abroad, and the international leader then manages the distributors.

Another example is when the leader of the program team for the political party hands over to the election coordinator, who then hands over to the leader of the party.

Ideally, all three leaders have been on the team from the start. The leader taking charge depends on the stage of the project. This way there is shared responsibility for success.

Now you are done with the Six Steps to Action, the strategy, and the **Six Steps strategic analysis team** hands over to the **implementation team**.

Organization and Handovers from Strategy Project to Implementation to Ongoing

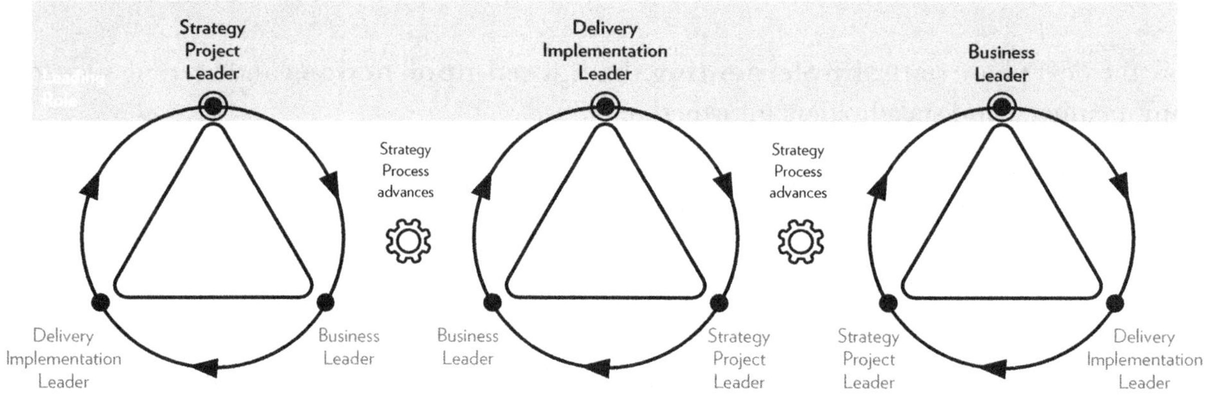

Figure 15. Responsibility changes as projects move from study to implementation and steady state

As the Strategy Process advances in your organization, it is recommended to have a complete team. As mentioned, make sure to have those in the team that will be charged with implementation and later leading the new situation. Different professionals will take a leading role during and after the process. When running the SIX STEPS the **Strategy Project Leader** will head the team. Once the Strategy has been agreed the **Delivery Implementation Leader** takes over implementing all the changes. Finally, when the organization is back in a stable state the **Business Leader** or **Head of the Organization** will be in charge. And…then the process starts again because change never ends!

PART C REFERENCES AND SOURCES

Books and articles mentioned in the book. The website *www.sixsteps-goals-action.com* section Tools and Techniques provides a list of suggested further reading.

Baggini, J. (2019). *How the World Thinks: A Global History of Philosophy*. Granta Books.

Carroll, L. (1865). *Alice's Adventures in Wonderland* and *Through the Looking-Glass*. https://ci.nii.ac.jp/ncid/BB29820787.

Cohen, W. (2012). *Drucker on Marketing: Lessons from the World's Most Influential Business Thinker*. McGraw Hill Professional.

Covey, S. R. (1997). The Seven Habits of Highly Effective People: Restoring the Character Ethic. Macmillan Reference USA.

Drucker, P. F. (1964). *Managing for Results* (1st ed.). William Heinemann Ltd.

Drucker, P. F. (1955, 2006). *The Practice of Management*. HarperBusiness.

Eischen, J. (2011). *Energy and the City: Career advice from senior executives. Misturafina Publishing*

Higgins, J. M. (2005). The Eight 'S's of Successful Strategy Execution. *Journal of Change Management*, *5*(1), 3–13. https://doi.org/10.1080/14697010500036064

Kay, J. (2011). "Those at the Nucleus May Not Have the Best View," John Kay.com. Accessed January 30, 2024, https://www.johnkay.com/2011/02/02/those-at-the-nucleus-may-not-have-the-best-view/.

Kay, J. (2006). *The Hare & the Tortoise: An Informal Guide to Business Strategy.* Erasmus Press Limited.

Minto, B. (2009). *The Pyramid Principle: Logic in Writing and Thinking*. Pearson Education.

Ohmae, K. (1982). *The Mind of the Strategist: The Art of Japanese Business*. New York: McGraw-Hill.

Van Der Veer, J. (2023). *Van A naar B: Lessen in Leiderschap*. Prometheus.

Wilde, Ó., & Hart-Davis, R. (1962). *The Letters of Oscar Wilde.* https://ci.nii.ac.jp/ncid/BA06881945

Figure 14.

You can only win a race with a good team and an agreed-upon plan of action: the strategy.

(Harvest Moon Regatta 2013)

SIX STEPS: THANKS

First, thanks to my wife, Joan Eischen, who, by writing her book *Energy and the City* and suggesting an accompanying website, kept me going on this project.

Many thanks to all the leaders and colleagues who have taught me to think and work strategically, and to all the students and team members who have asked good questions and motivated me to write this book.

I would like to give special mention and thanks to executives and friends that have taught me about strategy. Kors van Wyngaarden made me focus on the "Five Bullet Points," Oscar Fanjul gave me the opportunity to be an outsider learning to work in a different culture, Peter Buis knew when to disagree with me, Wayne Hutchinson and Greg Lewin made it possible for me to become a better dealmaker, and Jeroen van der Veer showed me early in my career how to simplify things and how to get from A to B.

Jan Edelman Bos asked me for the real key issue of the company where I did my master thesis and has transformed how I look at companies ever since. Gilbert Wawoe took the time as a senior executive to teach a young manager how to sell-in to multiple stakeholders. I am very thankful for shaping my analytical mindset and learning how to get ideas accepted by all the stakeholders.

The motivation to write the *Six Steps* has been provided by mentees and the students of EuroCollege and Erasmus University. Seeing how a better explanation worked and answering their questions convinced me of the need for a short and to-the-point set of actions to get to a strategy.

Meghan Fisher, Eline Nelis, Jalaja Ahuja, Bas Donkers, and Julian Henriot were most helpful in proofreading the manuscript, and their observations have made this a much better book than I could have written alone.

MAARTEN VAN HASSELT, BACKGROUND

Van Hasselt has built his career in leadership roles within major industrial companies, always focusing on creating profitable, long-term, sustainable value.

He has held integrated P&L and commercial line executive positions, and board memberships, as well as advisory roles in large consultancies and in his own company.

He excels at integrating varied, multicultural relationships to create strategies that deliver both locally and across large business areas.

He coaches team members for performance, shares his expertise, and is highly sought after as a mentor and career adviser. He serves as a visiting professor at Erasmus University, specializing in business economics and marketing strategy.

Maarten has an MBA and BSc in mechanical engineering (that explains the "Tool Kit"). He has also completed executive programs at MIT, INSEAD, and IMD. The Energy Institute has endorsed him as a Fellow (FEI). He is a Certified Champion Deal Leader (CCDL) and CRKBO licensed docent.

Maarten is fluent in Dutch, English, Spanish, German, and Portuguese, and has basic knowledge of French and Italian. This allows him to operate effectively locally and globally.

Having lived and worked in Latin America, Europe, and the United States for many years, and with projects in the Middle and Far East, Maarten has gained valuable experience and insights into different business cultures.

In addition to his professional accomplishments, Maarten is an experienced coastal yachtsman. He also coaches yacht owners on offshore safety.

TOOLS AND TECHNIQUES

Tools and Techniques are regularly updated and can be found on the website.

Sources and suggestions for further reading can be found on at:

www.sixsteps-goals-action.com

Made in United States
Orlando, FL
29 June 2026

82768158R00046